AUGUSTA SAVAGE

Sculptor of the Harlem Renaissance

Celebrating BLACK ARTISTS

AUGUSTA SAVAGE
Sculptor of the Harlem Renaissance

Enslow Publishing
101 W. 23rd Street
Suite 240
New York, NY 10011
USA
enslow.com

CHARLOTTE ETINDE-CROMPTON AND SAMUEL WILLARD CROMPTON

Published in 2020 by Enslow Publishing, LLC.
101 W. 23rd Street, Suite 240, New York, NY 10011

Copyright © 2020 by Enslow Publishing, LLC.

All rights reserved.

No part of this book may be reproduced by any means without the written permission of the publisher.

Library of Congress Cataloging-in-Publication Data

Names: Crompton, Samuel Willard, author. | Etinde-Crompton, Charlotte, author.
Title: Augusta Savage : sculptor of the Harlem Renaissance/Samuel Willard
  Crompton, Charlotte Etinde-Crompton.
Description: New York : Enslow Publishing, 2020. | Series: Celebrating
  black artists | Includes bibliographical references and index. | Audience: Grades
  7–12.
Identifiers: LCCN 2018015719| ISBN 9781978503618 (library bound) |
  ISBN 9781978505360 (pbk.)
Subjects: LCSH: Savage, Augusta, 1892–1962—Biography—Juvenile literature. |
  Sculptors—United States—Biography—Juvenile literature. | African American
  sculptors—Biography—Juvenile literature. | Harlem Renaissance—Juvenile
  literature.
Classification: LCC NB237.S286 C76 2019 | DDC 730.92 [B]—dc23
LC record available at https://lccn.loc.gov/2018015719

Printed in China

To Our Readers: We have done our best to make sure all website addresses in this book were active and appropriate when we went to press. However, the author and the publisher have no control over and assume no liability for the material available on those websites or on any websites they may link to. Any comments or suggestions can be sent by e-mail to customerservice@enslow.com.

Photo Credits: Cover, p 3 Archives of American Art/Wikimedia Commons/ File:Archives_of_American_Art_-_Augusta_Savage_-_2371/(17 U.S.C. §§ 101 and 105); pp. 7, 68 Everett Collection Inc./Alamy Stock Photo; p. 10 Stock Montage/ Archive Photos/Getty Images; pp. 14–15 Paul Fearn/Alamy Stock Photo; pp. 19, 22–23, 28–29 Smith Collection/Gado/Archive Photos/Getty Images; p. 25 C. M. Battey/Hulton Archive/Getty Images; pp. 26, 65 Hansel Mieth/The LIFE Picture Collection/Getty Images; p. 33 Universal Images Group/Getty Images; pp. 35, 60 Schomburg Center for Research in Black Culture/The New York Public Library; p. 40 nsf/Alamy Stock Photo; p. 42 New York Daily News/Getty Images; pp. 46–47 Michael Ochs Archives/Getty Images; p. 50 Cleveland Museum of Art, OH, USA/ Purchase from the J. H. Wade Fund/Bridgeman Images; p. 52 Library of Congress/ Corbis Historical/Getty Images; pp. 56–57 Apic/Hulton Archive/Getty Images; p. 58 U.S. National Archives and Records Administration; p. 71 ©Art Media/ Heritage-Images/The Image Works; pp. 76–77 The New York Public Library/Art Resource, NY; p. 79 Sherman Oaks Antique Mall/Archive Photos/Getty Images; pp. 84–85 Philip Scalia/Alamy Stock Photo; p. 87 Bettmann/Getty Images.

Contents

1 Soft Florida Clay 6

2 A Path Leading North 13

3 Schooling and Sculpting in New York City 21

4 A Rising Star 32

5 Heartbreak from Overseas 39

6 Harlem's Renaissance 45

7 An American in Paris 55

8 Teacher and Mentor 64

9 The World's Fair 74

10 An Unusual Retirement 82

Chronology 89

Chapter Notes 93

Glossary 97

Further Reading 99

Index 101

About the Authors 104

Soft Florida Clay

Does anyone know the precise moment at which an artist is "born"? Many painters, sculptors, and singers can identify the moment, saying it was when they first saw an easel, a pound of clay, or a working stage. Such stories help us understand the evolution of the artist. But the situation is distinctly more difficult for African American artists. Their white contemporaries struggle with many things, including the challenge to get their work recognized, but African Americans were oppressed for so long that many people believed it impossible for them ever to become great artists. That belief was and is, of course, thoroughly mistaken.

Making Art from Mud

Augusta Savage never tired of telling friends and acquaintances that she was a Leap Day baby, born Augusta Fells on February 29, 1892. She was born and raised in Green Cove Springs, a city 40 miles (64 kilometers) from Jacksonville, Florida. Green Cove Springs was a tourist locale, with many northerners who came south to enjoy the mild winters. But it was also a manufacturing city, where

From an early age, Augusta Savage developed an interest in crafting animal figures.

red clay bricks were produced. At an early age, Augusta played in the mud pits and used that Florida clay to shape figures, of animals and humans.

"At the mud pie age, I began to make 'things' instead of mud pies."[1] This is as close as Augusta Savage ever came to describing her moment of discovery, the precise time at which her artistic path was launched. If her memory was accurate, she came to self-recognition as an artist at a very early age. The soft red clay of northern Florida was her easel, her stage, and her performer's microphone, all rolled into one.

Throughout life, Savage displayed ambivalence about her upbringing. To some friends, she boasted of her father, Edward, a hard-working man who owned 15 acres (6 hectares) of land in their hometown. To others, Savage confided that her childhood had been very difficult. And the reason was not hard to find.

Edward Fells earned a meager living as a house painter, but he was also an assistant pastor at the local Methodist church. A true fundamentalist, Fells disliked what his daughter did: he saw her clay figures as examples of what the Bible calls the worship of graven images. His disapproval of his daughter's art eventually translated into severe physical punishment.

How frequently did Edward beat his daughter? Perhaps as much as four times a week. By the time she was ten, Augusta Savage had practically all the art beaten out of her, as she later declared. Her father's behavior is horrifying to our modern ears, but it was not atypical for that time. Early-twentieth-century parents believed it their duty to beat their children when necessary, to rescue them from the error of their ways.

Early Economic Hardship

"I was born in Florida of poor parents."[2] These are the opening words of Augusta Savage's brief autobiography, penned for *The Crisis*, the leading African American periodical of the 1920s. In many ways, this short summation of her early circumstances said it all. In 1929, for a person to describe herself as black, poor, and living in Florida was quite sufficient. Almost everyone got the picture.

Florida had been part of the Confederate States of America. Its long history, which commenced with Spanish rule, was filled with slavery, poverty, and oppression. The typical *Crisis* reader, therefore, understood just what Augusta Savage meant. But she went further: "I am the seventh child in a family of fourteen. Nine of us reached maturity."[3] Contemporary readers may be appalled by the low survival rate, but *Crisis* readers were not. They knew that African Americans had a lower survival rate on average and that the rate of survival of those that lived in the Deep South was even worse. For the discerning *Crisis* reader of 1929, it was apparent that Savage and her family had a rather hard road in life.

Crisis readers went on to discover that when Savage first arrived in New York City, she had all of $4.60 in her pocket. This was not as unusual, or sensational, as it would be in our time. But it does indicate she was part of the Great Migration, the movement of hundreds of thousands of African Americans from the Deep South to the urban North.

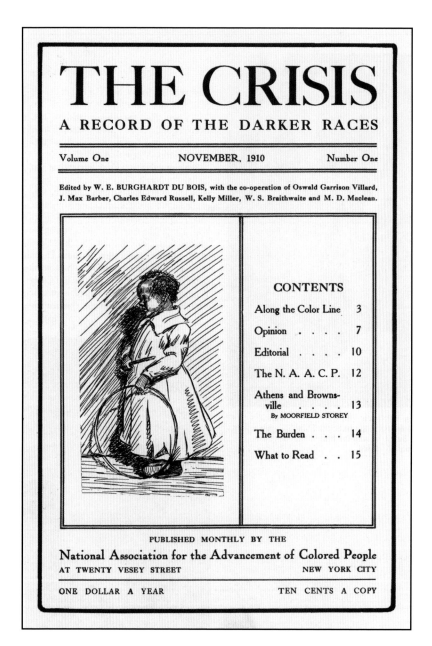

Created in 1910 by W. E. B. Du Bois, *The Crisis* was the leading news and opinion publication for black Americans.

Biblical Fundamentalism

Today we employ the words "fundamentalism" and "fundamentalist" a great deal. The meaning they possess comes from the early twentieth century, the very time when Savage grew up in northern Florida. The fundamentalist movement derives its name from publication of *The Fundamentals,* a series of pamphlet-books issued between 1910 and 1915.

The First Move

The Fells family remained in Green Cove Springs until 1906 or 1907. This was, coincidentally, just about the high point for the city and vicinity—the time when the tourist trade was most successful. But the African American population was left out of the move toward prosperity. Postcards that survive show blacks as waiters and cooks, and occasionally as amateur musicians, but never as successful, middle-class citizens.[4] Augusta and her family were not sad to leave. Edward Fells had gained a full-time pastoral position in a Methodist church in West Palm Beach. The family moved 350 miles (563 km) south, and their material circumstances improved. A new life beckoned.

Whether Augusta moved with her family is not certain. She married John Moore, a carpenter, just as her family was moving in 1907, when she was fifteen years old. The couple had a daughter they named Irene, but Moore died soon afterward. Augusta may have even stayed in Green

12 AUGUSTA SAVAGE: *Sculptor of the Harlem Renaissance*

Cove Springs until her husband passed away. But she did later rejoin the full family and spent her late teen years in West Palm Beach. It was around this time that Augusta came back to her art.

Legend has it that Augusta was riding in a wagon with Mr. Milkens, principal of the local high school, when she saw a local potter's barn. Augusta was eager for an opportunity to work with art materials, and going inside, she petitioned for some clay. She had plenty of natural clay back home in Green Cove Springs, but West Palm Beach was quite different: sand prevailed over clay. Lacking her chosen material, Savage had gone years without sculpting any figures. Now, however, she asked for clay and was handed a bucket that held 25 pounds (11 kilograms). Over the next forty-eight hours, she sculpted her first figure in many years.

When she was finished, Savage brought the 18-inch-high (46 centimeter) figurine to her father. Much to Reverend Fells's surprise, his daughter had sculpted a figure of the Virgin Mary. She declared her desire to accomplish great art in God's service. Her father was won over, and her pursuit of art, blocked for so many years, now began afresh.

Chapter

2

A Path Leading North

Soon after sculpting the Virgin Mary, Augusta turned wholeheartedly to her art. Perhaps all was not forgiven between her and her father, but the family returned to a normal unit.

The Fells family did better in West Palm Beach than in Green Cove Springs. Their path was seldom easy, however. Less is known than one would like, but it seems certain that one of Augusta's brothers served with the US Army in the First World War. He returned home safely, but the family made one sacrifice after another.

There was one other major occurrence during this time, around 1915: Augusta Savage, then still known as Augusta Fells, married a carpenter, James Savage. Though the marriage ended in divorce in the early 1920s, it did leave an enduring mark upon Savage: she retained his last name throughout her life.

As for her career, Savage was alert for opportunities to show off more of her work. She saw the Palm Beach Fair as the single best outlet for her creative energies. Palm Beach was in its early development, and the fair was its major

14   AUGUSTA SAVAGE: *Sculptor of the Harlem Renaissance*

Many parts of Green Cove Springs, Florida, were picturesque, but there was an undeniable lack of opportunity for black residents.

exhibition of its value, a means by which the city could "sell" itself to northern investors. The Palm Beach County Fair was meant to showcase the talents and energies of native-born Floridians, but, in one of the ironies of that time, it was presided over by an outsider, a migrant from the North.

An Unexpected Connection

Born in Quebec, Canada, in 1867, George Graham Currie was not anyone's idea of an angel or savior. A burly Scotts-Canadian, he had come south decades earlier with just pennies in his pocket. Through grit, hard work, and a healthy measure of luck, he rose to become mayor of Palm Beach. Currie also served as superintendent of the county fair, and, as such, he was in a special position to help Savage.

When Savage approached to ask for a favor, Currie was skeptical. No previous African American had advertised at the fair, and he anticipated pushback from the community. But the more the two conversed, the more intrigued Currie became. How, he wondered, had this untutored young woman accomplished so much? And when he agreed to the request, granting Savage a booth to display her art, his faith was more than justified. She won a $25 prize and subscriptions were raised, bringing her total to $175, an almost unheard of amount for an African American female. Deeply affected by this surprising success, Savage wrote a poem to Currie:

As the Forks of Life's great highway
I approach,
And the hour of my temptation
is at hand;
In my soul's Gethsemane,
I have still *your* faith in me
And it strengthens me to know
You understand.[1]

Though the poetry is affecting and shows Savage's talent beyond visual art, the reader must wonder, however, what she meant by "In my soul's Gethsemane." The more one ponders the situation, the more likely it seems that she was contemplating leaving her daughter, Irene, with her parents. If so, then the "hour of my temptation" refers to the painful choice she had to make between devoted motherhood and devotion to her art.

Not to be outdone, Currie composed a poem of his own. Noting that Savage was a poet, as well as a sculptor, he wrote of the effect of her work.

Augusta is a sculptress fine—
A poetess as well:
Her coal black hair and eyes that shine
A soulful story tell.
Her agile step, her lithesome grace.
Her happy carefree mien;
Proclaim her o'er her swarthy race
A veritable queen….
With steady eye she looks on me,
Then takes a lump of clay:
When lo! Another self I see—
With all my faults away.[2]

Given that Currie was then known as "Florida's poet," this was no small praise.

Mother and Daughter

The intricacies of Augusta Savage's relationship with her daughter–her only living child–remain murky at best. Did Irene Moore feel abandoned by her mother? Was it merely coincidence that Augusta left her when Irene was fourteen years old, at almost the very age when Augusta had married John Moore? All we can say for certain is that there must have remained a certain level of warmth between mother and daughter, as Irene looked after and cared for Augusta in her old age.

Natives and New Arrivals

Florida has long been a playful battleground between the native-born and those who arrive as adults. Currie was part of a migration from Canada that commenced near the end of the nineteenth century and continues right into our own time. Savage was a true native, but her African American status meant she needed a patron, and Currie proved just the right person. The social and political contest between various ethnic groups, as well as native-born and "outsiders," continues.

The Second Move

The chronology of Savage's life is often uncertain. She did not make it easy, either for her admirers or biographers. Sometimes she shaved a full decade off her years and, remarkably, got away with the deception. We are reasonably confident, however, that she studied at Florida Normal Teachers College in Tallahassee for a time, and that—discontent with her academic studies—she moved to Jacksonville.

"I hoped to 'do' the busts of all our rich colored people there," Savage wrote, "and so make enough money to finance my art career."[3] To the best of our knowledge, Savage was turned down by almost every person or family she approached. The rejection seems cruel to us in

A Path Leading North

retrospect, but to the well-to-do African American families, it made perfect sense. If they did commission a bust, they would surely seek a well-known sculptor with academic credentials. This was something that Savage simply did not have.

Augusta Savage did not plan to become part of the Great Migration. But without any better options, she had no choice but to leave Florida. Precisely how she financed the trip remains uncertain, but she caught a bus all the way from Jacksonville to New York City. Shortly before departure, she visited her old hometown of Green Cove Springs and composed a poem that was published two years later.

Savage worked on her art while residing in the town of Jacksonville, Florida, but it wasn't long before she set out for a much bigger city.

> I visited today the old Homestead,
> Deserted now for many busy years,
> Explored again with memory laden tread,
> The birthplace of so many hopes and fears.[4]

The fears are readily apparent. Savage had endured terrible beatings at her father's hand, all for the "crime" of making figures from clay. But the hopes were real, too, and the modern student may struggle to understand how she came by her propensity for art. She had little if any exposure to high art, yet the desire was there almost from the very beginning.

> And down my time scarred cheek there crept a tear,
> For those who sleep beneath the ocean's foam,
> And then a sigh for other hearts so dear
> That rest so gently 'neath the sand of home.[5]

There was poetic license involved, but also a measure of fact. Savage had already lost five brothers and sisters, and others would perish in a terrible Florida hurricane a few years later.

But as Savage took that fateful bus ride, she would not just be leaving behind the joys and pains of the homestead of her youth—she was blazing a new path in Manhattan.

Chapter

3

Schooling and Sculpting in New York City

Augusta Savage arrived in Manhattan sometime in 1921, and she almost immediately found living quarters in Harlem. She did not expect, or anticipate, the rich cultural scene she found.

Located between 95th and 140th Streets, Harlem was the heart of New York City's African American community. Two decades earlier, it had been home to many white people but most had left, and by 1921, Harlem was the unofficial "capital" of black America. Perhaps two hundred thousand African Americans lived in Harlem, and by 1922 they were the most cohesive black group in the entire nation. They were cohesive in their goals—meaning they wanted to elevate the condition of blacks everywhere. Ethnically, they were a fascinating amalgam, with African Americans from the Deep South and West Indian blacks from Jamaica and Cuba. Nearly all these black people agreed America was

22 AUGUSTA SAVAGE: *Sculptor of the Harlem Renaissance*

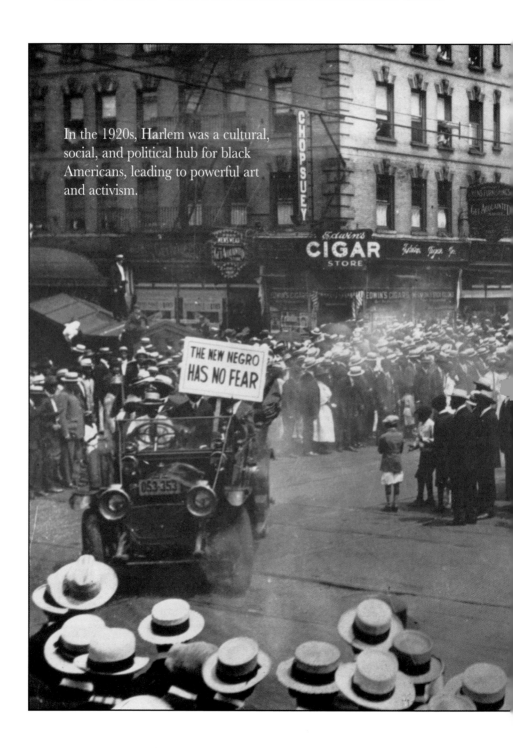

In the 1920s, Harlem was a cultural, social, and political hub for black Americans, leading to powerful art and activism.

Schooling and Sculpting in New York City

An Intellectual Leader

Born in western Massachusetts in 1869, William Edward Burghardt Du Bois—best known as W. E. B. Du Bois—was the proud leader of the intellectual African American community. His brilliance was apparent to all. The first black person to earn a PhD from Harvard, Du Bois taught sociology at Atlanta University before coming north to Manhattan, where he edited *The Crisis*, the number one periodical for African Americans in the 1920s. Du Bois had a complicated picture of how black people had arrived at their circumstances, but his vision for the future was startlingly simple. All great peoples and nations depend on their most talented members, Du Bois declared. A select few, the "Talented Tenth" or 10 percent, would be the ones to lead black Americans forward toward a brighter, more equal future.

How Augusta Savage and W. E. B. Du Bois first met is not known, but by 1922, Savage and Du Bois were acquainted. The great leader took a strong liking to the newly arrived southerner, and by the end of the 1920s, they were exchanging letters as Savage was settling in to a new studio in Paris.

Schooling and Sculpting in New York City 25

An influential thinker, writer, and leader, W. E. B. Du Bois believed that a select group of educated, gifted black citizens would lead the way forward.

Augusta Savage began her formal artistic training at Cooper Union in the fall of 1921.

a deeply racist society, intent on holding them back. The great majority of them believed in action: social, economic, and artistic.

Cooper Union

Immediately upon arriving in Harlem, Savage visited the home of sculptor Solon Borglum. One of America's finest sculptors, his brother was the artist who later carved the monumental heads at Mount Rushmore, South Dakota.

Savage had a letter of recommendation from George Graham Currie, but Borglum quickly burst her bubble. He did take on young students, Borglum explained, but they were children of the wealthy who paid very large fees. There was not the slightest chance Savage could afford them. Seeing her despair, Borglum suggested she apply to Cooper Union, a nearby college. Located in the lower part of Manhattan, Cooper Union did not charge tuition.

Hours later, Savage was at Cooper Union. She found that more than 140 other young people were on the waiting list for admission. Luckily, Savage somehow won first the attention and then the admiration of Kate L. Reynolds, superintendent of the school. Showing Reynolds a bust she had recently executed in plaster, Savage gained admittance to the school. Her formal studies in art commenced in October 1921.

Another Roadblock

Savage did extremely well at Cooper Union. Somehow, she completed the first year of sculptural study in roughly six weeks. Her natural talent was obvious, and if she had a weakness, it was a stubborn determination to execute her subjects in her own way, rather than by established method.

That she would complete the program seemed a sure thing. But in February 1922, Savage's funds ran dry. She worked as a laundress, somehow managing to balance physical work with her art studies. But she could not afford to eat, much less to purchase artistic materials. Now possessing a deep investment in Savage's work, Kate Reynolds came to the rescue. She found her work at a well-to-do home, and she convened a special meeting of the Cooper Union board. Recognizing Savage's exceptional skill, the board voted to raise funds for all her materials and expenses. This was truly extraordinary, as no previous student had ever received this assistance.

With the roadblock removed, Savage continued to work. She labored as a laundress, studied at Cooper Union, and found time to execute a bust of W. E. B. Du Bois, the central figure of the intellectual movement in Harlem. The bust was an outstanding success. Du Bois was a handsome man, but his intensity sometimes led to his being caricatured. Not in this case. Augusta Savage

Schooling and Sculpting in New York City

The New York Public Library on 135th Street became the home for the W.E.B. Du Bois bust, until its theft in 1960.

AUGUSTA SAVAGE: *Sculptor of the Harlem Renaissance*

The Du Bois Bust

For almost three decades, the bust of W. E. B. Du Bois was one of the features of the New York Public Library on 135th Street. Tens of thousands, perhaps even hundreds of thousands, of visitors and patrons gazed on the fine features brought to life by Augusta Savage. But the bust was stolen around the year 1960. Those who wanted to impugn Savage's reputation claimed that she was involved—even that she paid the person who stole the bust. Though Savage and Du Bois did part ways over the years and admiration may have turned to resentment, this outrageous claim was never proved.

captured Du Bois so well that "Militancy, intelligence, and resolve are present in every plane."[1]

That Savage had a difficult path to success makes the bloom of her creativity and skill in New York all the more admirable. The African American journalist Eric Walrond captured her life thusly: "She lives in a poorly lighted room in Upper Harlem," Walrond wrote, "and while putting the finishing touches to a bust she is making...told me the story of her life."[2] Walrond went on to recount many parts of Savage's story, including the move from Florida to New York City. That Savage contended with all manner of difficulties was beyond dispute: that she pushed forward regardless was also undoubtedly true. Walrond concluded his essay with "Certainly we have another sculptress we can gloriously be proud of."[3]

Schooling and Sculpting in New York City   31

Eric Walrond could not have been more correct: Augusta Savage's superior artistry was worthy of significant praise. Her talent would go a long way toward explaining how she was able to sculpt both of the towering geniuses of her time; having completed the Du Bois likeness, the bust she was working on as Walrond interviewed her was of another major figure in the black American community: Marcus Garvey.

Chapter 4

A Rising Star

As with W. E. B. Du Bois, the circumstances of Augusta Savage first encountering Marcus Garvey are unknown. Whether she met him at one of his rallies in Harlem or through one of his aides, she started work on a bust of Garvey in 1922.

Garvey presented a much more difficult subject than Du Bois. Whereas Du Bois had the head of an aristocrat, a person born to lead, Garvey had far less patrician features. Not only was Garvey overweight, but he also had small eyes, which, even in photographs, do not convey his immense oratorical power. How does an artist convey the power of *sound*—that of Garvey's voice?

Savage pulled it off. The Garvey bust shows the incredible power of the man. Savage plays his small eyes true but uses the back of the neck to convey Garvey's sensational power. Much admired by the Garvey family, the bust has remained in their possession in Jamaica—Garvey's home country—ever since. Was there any other artist who could move between the Du Bois and Garvey camps? None that we know of.

A Rising Star

While W. E. B. Du Bois was a talented scholar and writer, Marcus Garvey stunned audiences with his powerful, stirring speeches.

Battle for the Soul

In 1922, the African American community was torn between two great leaders and competing visions. Many black Americans admired the ideas of W. E. B. Du Bois, but an equal number were thrilled by the speeches of Marcus Garvey. Unlike the Massachusetts native Du Bois, Garvey was not African American. Born on the island of Jamaica in 1886, he was Caribbean African. But when he first came to Manhattan in 1916, Garvey struck a chord with many black American citizens.

Two men more different are hard to imagine. Though he was not a scholarly thinker like Du Bois, Garvey was a fantastic speaker. Garvey was the ultimate populist, playing to the masses with parades, marching bands, and dramatic speeches. His talks, delivered to sold-out crowds in Harlem, called for a "Back to Africa" movement. Garvey wanted to resettle African Americans in Africa, but he also wanted to improve their material conditions right away. His followers organized some of the first successful black economic actions. Du Bois was the ultimate ivory tower intellectual, writing, philosophizing, and criticizing. He turned his critical eye toward Garvey's arguments and positions, picking apart their flaws, while ignoring the flaws of his own. These two men competed for the soul of the African American future.

Savage's third husband, Robert Poston, was a journalist and editor who worked on the *Negro World* newspaper with his brother, Ulysses.

A Third Chance at Love

Sometime in 1922, perhaps at the same time she met Marcus Garvey, Augusta Savage fell in love for the third time. The expression "the third time's the charm" was accurate in this case.

Born in Hopkinsville, Kentucky, in 1890, Robert L. Poston was a black journalist just one year Savage's senior. Like Savage, he came from a large family: he was the second-eldest child of eight. His schoolteacher parents endowed Poston with a powerful sense of social responsibility.

Also like Augusta Savage, Robert Poston knew tragedy. His mother died young, and he had already lost three siblings to illness and sudden death. Seeking to make the most of what he imagined would be a short life, Poston moved to Detroit, where he and a younger brother edited a newspaper aimed at African Americans. By 1922, both brothers lived in Harlem, where they worked for the Marcus Garvey–led movement advocating black nationalism. In the course of working on the Garvey bust, Savage fell deeply in love with Poston, and in October of 1923, the pair married.

The Fontainebleau Affair

Even aside from this latest marriage, 1923 was a landmark year for Savage. She applied for admission to the Fontainebleau School of Fine Arts in France, sending photographs of her best sculptures and paintings. But even before she sent her full application fee, Savage learned she was rejected. The committee, composed of leading American artists and intellectuals, explained that they turned down Savage's application on the basis of her race, concerned that her inclusion wouldn't be well regarded by the white American students who would be attending the school.

Frustrated by this unfair turn of events, Savage took her case to the Harlem newspapers. To her surprise, the case was soon taken to the white press, too, and her name became known nationwide. Very likely, it was her deepening relationship with journalist Robert Poston that provided contact with different newspapers. But however she gained this access, no one could deny that Savage argued her case well.

"I don't care much for myself," Savage wrote, "but other and better colored students might wish to apply sometime. This is the first year the school is open and I am the first colored girl to apply. I don't like to see them establish a precedent...How am I to compete with other American artists if I am not given the same opportunity?"[1] This was hard to argue. Savage went on to say that one of her brothers was "good enough" to serve in the US military in World War I and to fight in France, while she was not seen as good enough even to study art in that same country.

Savage also took her opinion to a forum held in Harlem. "I wanted to go so badly," she declared, "that I worked night and day and bought new clothes so that I would look all right. I was much surprised when they told me I was a little too dark. I am the only colored girl in my class at Cooper Union and the others look on me as though I were a freak."[2] The Fontainebleau affair dragged on all during the spring and summer of 1923. Prominent Americans even asked President Warren G. Harding to intervene. But in the end, nothing was done.

In spite of this professional setback, Savage won a moral victory. Hundreds of thousands of newspaper readers sympathized with her and decried the decision of the arts committee. But still, many art and cultural leaders around the United States decided that Augusta Savage was a troublemaker and chose to avoid her—and her work—in the future.

A New Mission

Savage and Poston were married in October 1923. Just weeks later, Poston learned he had been selected for a very important task: he was one of four delegates chosen to represent Marcus Garvey and the Garvey movement on a mission to Liberia, in West Africa, to discuss resettlement of black Americans. The honor was apparent to all. But the timing could not have been worse; by the time Robert Poston went aboard the SS *President Grant*, headed for Africa, he knew that his wife was pregnant.

Chapter 5

Heartbreak from Overseas

By December 1923, Robert Poston was the number two man in the Garvey movement. Handsome, educated, and articulate, Poston was the only person who could conceivably be seen as a successor to Garvey. In addition to all of her other accomplishments, Augusta Savage was also, therefore, one of the leading ladies of the Garvey movement.

A New Life

Savage had only been pregnant once before and that was nearly fifteen years earlier. So she viewed her condition with trepidation as well as joy. Things did not become easier when her husband boarded the ship, headed for Liberia. Though she had plenty of acquaintances in Harlem, few of them were close friends. Savage had endured so much loss and significant betrayal that she was reluctant to trust anyone very deeply. There were two consolations, however. The first was that her husband had been so powerfully honored. The second was the expectation that she would soon become a mother.

40 AUGUSTA SAVAGE: *Sculptor of the Harlem Renaissance*

Though 1924 was a year of devastating loss for Augusta Savage, she continued to work on her art.

The Thunderclap

On March 16, 1924, Marcus Garvey gave two speeches in Manhattan. The first was to a large out-of-doors crowd in Harlem, and the other was to a sold-out crowd in Madison Square Garden.

Rising to deliver the second speech, Garvey knew that he—and the movement—were in serious trouble. White Americans showed alarm at his strident tone, and there were FBI agents in the crowd, taking in every word. Garvey was a seasoned orator, however, and he commenced his speech in fine style.

The news from Liberia was good, even excellent, Garvey declared. The president of Liberia had offered a wide stretch of land—there was room enough for all those that wanted to settle there. The news in America was equally good, Garvey asserted. Movement efforts had resulted in better wages for African American workers. In the middle of this optimistic state of the union, Garvey was suddenly interrupted. An aide handed him a radiogram, and Garvey stopped his speech to read it aloud: Robert Poston was dead. Aboard the SS *President Grant*, Poston was hurrying home from Africa when he contracted and died of double pneumonia.

Many people in the audience wept.

From Roses to Ashes

Just five months earlier, Augusta Savage had become a bride. Now, in March 1924, she was a widow. Savage had experienced several turns of fortune in life, but this was the single most dramatic and perhaps the most painful.

Garvey's impending prison sentence cut short his leadership and altered the course of the political movement he started.

When her husband's body was brought ashore, the pregnant Savage and other Universal Negro Improvement League (UNIL) members arranged for a special railroad car to bring him to Hopkinsville, Kentucky. Many years later, the members of the city's black community would recall the great significance of the event.

A Dream of Africa Fades

With a prison sentence for mail fraud looming on the horizon, Garvey's movement in America faded in less than a year's time from his 1924 speech. A tentative agreement between the Universal Negro Improvement League and the Republic of Liberia for possible resettlement died a quick death. But while resettlement eluded him, Marcus Garvey is justly regarded as the man "who dared to fail." His failed mission of the early 1920s was later resurrected by Malcolm X and other African American leaders of the 1960s.

"Flowers? I had never *seen* so many flowers,"[1] one lady recalled. "Here was one of us who had come into a national movement," another one remembered. "[He had] been to Africa, and in the process of trying to liberate the people. A great wreath made in the shape of a floral clock showed the hour at which he passed. It was a historical event for us."[2]

Augusta Savage became an instant hero to Hopkinsville's black community. Some wished her to remain in town, but Savage was too committed to the arts community in Harlem. She did remain in Hopkinsville for a time, however, and she became fast friends with Ted Poston, the youngest sibling in her husband's family. Once this friendship was kindled, it endured for life.

The chronology of Savage's life is so uncertain that we are not certain whether she returned to Harlem in time for the birth or whether the baby was born in Hopkinsville. We do know that the birth was in June 1924 and that Savage named her new daughter Roberta, in her husband's honor. It appeared that something good had come from all the sacrifice and loss.

Unfortunately, this, too, would be taken. Just a few days after her birth, Roberta Savage Poston died. Augusta Savage was now three times married and had lost all three husbands—two to natural causes and one to divorce. She was now a bereaved parent as well.

While this loss was likely devastating and the pain enormous, Augusta Savage did not give up hope. Her personal story was filled with wreck and ruin, but the story of her art remained to be told.

Chapter **6**

Harlem's Renaissance

By the mid-1920s, Augusta Savage's life had certainly been eventful. She had already experienced three marriages, the birth of two children, and any number of hardships and difficulties. But Savage made the most of every opportunity that came her way. Now in her thirties, she witnessed enough of the Harlem Renaissance to know she wanted to get aboard that artistic and cultural train.

A Reunion with Du Bois

In 1923, Savage sculpted busts of both Marcus Garvey and W. E. B. Du Bois. By 1926, Garvey was in federal prison for mail fraud and he would soon be deported. This left Du Bois the unquestioned leader of the African American community.

Du Bois was a formidable, even stern, person. Many African American efforts—whether artistic or in the world of business—earned his disproval. This was not the case with Augusta Savage, however. Du Bois held her in the highest regard.

In the summer of 1926, Du Bois delivered the opening address to a convocation of the National Association for the Advancement of Colored People (NAACP). Choosing art as the centerpiece of his speech, Du Bois acknowledged that there would be critics, those who said art was a luxury most black people could not afford. To the contrary, Du Bois declared, art was essential.

The world of art held a special opportunity for African Americans, Du Bois declared. Having gone without the comforts enjoyed by many of their white countrymen, African Americans had something special to give the world of art, and they had a special ability to profit from it. Though he did not call Augusta Savage by name, it is completely clear that she was whom he meant by these words:

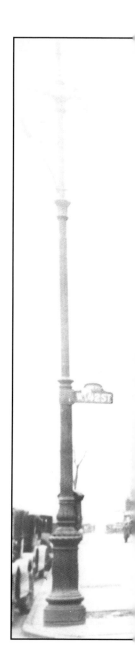

> There is in New York tonight a black woman molding clay by herself in a little bare room, because there is not a single school of sculpture in New York where she is welcome. Surely there are doors she might burst through, but when God makes a sculptor He does not always make the pushing sort of person who beats his way through doors thrust in his face. This girl is working her hands off *to get out of this country* so that she can get some sort of training[1] (emphasis added).

Harlem's Renaissance

The vibrancy of Harlem's cultural scene inspired Augusta Savage to continue sculpting, even in spite of her personal losses.

Touching on Savage's continued desire to study in Europe, Du Bois went on to explicate his theory of the importance of art. "All art is propaganda and ever must be, despite the wailings of the purists…I do not care a damn for any art that is not used for propaganda. But I do care when propaganda is confined to one side, while the other is stripped and silent."[2] Savage and Du Bois did not always agree, but in this belief, they were united.

Talent Amid Turmoil

Du Bois helped Savage obtain an artist's fellowship to the Royal Academy of Fine Arts in Rome. Delighted, Savage continued to work as a laundress, saving her money for the time of departure. But whatever she saved was wiped

Purists and Propaganda

Purists—whether of Augusta Savage's time or our own—insist on the distinctiveness and separateness of art. Every painting or piece of sculpture stands on its own and must be judged in that light. Those who speak of propaganda in art assert that each piece of art goes out from its creator and inevitably assumes other messages. Purists lament when art is used for a political message. Propagandists shake their head at purists, wondering how they can be so naïve. The debate was not settled in Savage's lifetime, and the chances are it will not be resolved in our own.

out when she brought her parents (her father was now disabled, through paralysis) north from Florida. Just as they settled in, Savage accepted another responsibility. One of her brothers died while rescuing flood victims in Florida, and his wife and children came north. By the late 1920s, there were nine people living in Savage's small apartment.

The close quarters led to tragedy. The circumstances are not well known but Savage's father—the stern minister who had once beat her regularly—died in her apartment, presumably from a kitchen fire.

During this difficult period, Savage had one unvarnished success. In 1926, she brought several of her sculptures to Baltimore, to exhibit them in the Federation of Parent Teacher Clubs. Her talent was seen by a mixed audience, including many white Americans. But Savage's biggest work was yet to come.

Gamin

Sometime in 1927 or 1928, Savage began sculpting the head and shoulders of a Harlem street boy ("urchin" is the less flattering term). Ever since the bust was unveiled in 1929, various people have claimed that they were the model. Some believe that the journalist Ted Poston—Savage's brother-in-law—was the inspiration for this piece of work. Others assert that the honor goes to Savage's nephew. Still others claim that a boy in Saugerties, New York, was the model. Despite all these assertions, no one person has ever proven his claim. The best that we can do is examine the work itself.

Modeled in bronze, *Gamin* brings to life a street boy, one whose face resembles that of hundreds, even thousands,

50　AUGUSTA SAVAGE: *Sculptor of the Harlem Renaissance*

Gamin (1929) remains one of Savage's most famous and celebrated works.

of young boys of the late 1920s. The boy, who looks to be thirteen or fourteen, wears a cap that is tilted upward, granting a jaunty feeling to the sculpture. But this is a deception, one that the viewer soon sees through. One need only look at the sad eyes, one of which is fully open while the other is half-closed. Here is a boy who has experienced real sadness. He is wise beyond his years.

The prominent nose achieves a breakthrough for the artistic sensibility as Savage seeks to accurately and reverently portray black physiognomy. Here, Savage has captured the spirit of the African American boy, he who makes his way through life by sheer grit, gumption, and sleight of hand. If this boy has a universal counterpart, one who belongs to all ethnicities and none at the same time, it is Aladdin, the Arab boy who carried a magic lamp.

Gazing down at the shoulders and chest, the viewer sees signs of malnourishment. This boy is not starving, but he knows what hunger is. If not for his street smarts, which echo through the entire piece, he would not have made it to this age.

How will this boy fare? Will he grow to become a family man, a starving artist, or perhaps a gangster? All of these possibilities are shown through Savage's exquisite work. *Gamin* was, and remains, her single most revealing and tantalizing piece of work. As one examines this sculpture, the mind naturally turns to the words of W. E. B. Du Bois: "all art is propaganda and ever must be, despite the wailings of the purists."

Few pieces of art ever received so immediate a reception.

Through his foundation, Julius Rosenwald supported the work of several black artists and writers.

The Reception

Gamin was immediately hailed as an artistic sensation and a breakthrough for Savage's career. A photograph was soon on the cover of *Opportunity* magazine, and Savage, quite suddenly, became the best-known artist in Harlem. *Gamin* revived her desire to travel abroad; indeed, reception of the bust made it possible.

During this time, W. E. B. Du Bois continued to work on Savage's behalf. In 1929, he informed her that the Julius Rosenwald Foundation was open to applications, and Savage soon applied for—and received—a one-year fellowship that finally enabled her to travel to France.

The Rosenwald Foundation

Julius Rosenwald (1862-1932) was born in Springfield, Illinois, the hometown of Abraham Lincoln. Keenly conscious of Lincoln's legacy, Rosenwald became a leading philanthropist. After making a fortune working with Sears, Roebuck and Company, Rosenwald endowed the Julius Rosenwald Foundation, which provides financial grants to individuals. In addition to Augusta Savage, the foundation also funded other prominent black artists and luminaries like Langston Hughes, Maya Angelou, and Savage's champion, W. E. B. Du Bois.

Preparations for Savage's European sojourn neared their end in the fall of 1929. Savage attended several parties thrown in her honor, parties at which her friends raised money for her trip. The Rosenwald grant was enough to meet her basic needs, but she needed other funds to purchase the many necessities, including art supplies. Her peers were all too happy to lend their support. By October of that year, Augusta Savage was in Paris.

Chapter **7**

An American in Paris

Augusta Savage seldom, if ever, experienced comfort, ease, or well-being. To the age of thirty-eight, she had experienced considerable hardship and difficulty. But the Rosenwald grant, and her subsequent travel to France, altered the circumstances of her life in a major way.

The City of Lights

Savage arrived in Paris early in 1930 and found the City of Lights was all it was cracked up to be. This city had proven to be a friend to visual artists, writers, and musicians for generations, and African Americans were the newest crop of foreigners to fall in love with the city on the River Seine.

Savage came to the city bearing a letter of introduction to Henry O. Tanner, who was then the most renowned of all African American painters. Arrangements had also been made so she could temporarily take over the studio apartment of African American sculptor Nancy Elizabeth Prophet. All told, things were set up to give Savage every encouragement and every possibility.

In 1929, after receiving the Rosenwald grant, Augusta Savage finally reached Paris.

By November 1929, Savage was enrolled at the Académie de la Grande Chaumière. She had private sessions with artist Félix Benneteau-Desgrois, who had previously won the First Grand Prize in Rome. In a letter to the Rosenwald Foundation, the French sculptor expressed

An American in Paris

confidence in his American pupil, declaring that she was very artistic and that with some luck, her models would be shown at the 1930 Paris Salon. At about the same time, Savage wrote home, saying that Monsieur Benneteau-Desgrois was very patient with her and that he constantly encouraged her work.

Yet Savage did not remain at Benneateau-Desgrois's studio. The precise reasons are unknown. One suspects, however, that Savage found a teacher who wanted her to pursue a particular preordained path. This had never been her style.

Savage again wrote home: "I have lately been trying to develop an original technique…but I find that the masters are not in sympathy as they all have their own definite ideas and usually wish their pupils to follow their particular method, so I have been working alone for the past three or four months only calling in a critic for suggestions."[1]

It's possible that this was a mistake. That Savage possessed great natural talent is undeniable. That she could have profited from a master's instruction is equally apparent. But what she lost in terms of formal art instruction, Savage

58 AUGUSTA SAVAGE: Sculptor of the Harlem Renaissance

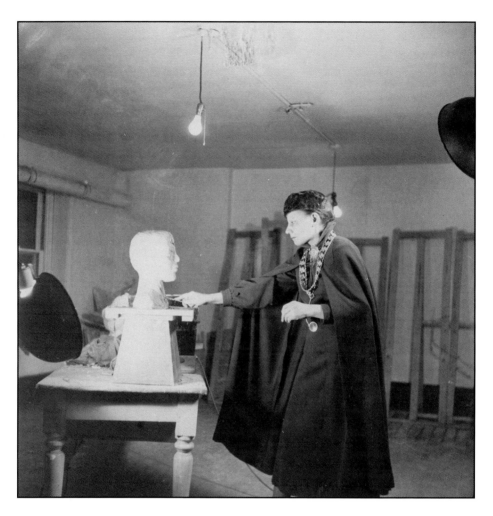

Like Augusta Savage, Nancy Elizabeth Prophet was a talented young black sculptor who thrived in Paris.

Nancy Elizabeth Prophet

Born and raised in Rhode Island, Nancy Elizabeth Prophet (1890–1960) was black and Native American: her father was a Narragansett Indian. Largely self-taught, Prophet moved to Paris in 1922 and remained in France for twelve years; her diary indicates she suffered severe depression during much of that time. Her artistic output was considerable, however; her well-regarded *Negro Head* was carved while she was in Paris. Prophet and Savage were very different people, but they shared one important aspect: both were African American women seeking to forge an artistic path and gain recognition in Paris during a time when few opportunities were available to them.

gained in terms of artistic independence. Working on her own, with materials purchased by Rosenwald funds, she turned out a handful of notable sculptures during her time in France.

Inspired by Dance

Though Savage kept no diary of her time in Paris, one suspects she occasionally found time to visit some of the world-renowned theatres. There, she may have seen some of the latest innovations in dance, some of which came from a fellow American woman, Isadora Duncan. Looking at

AUGUSTA SAVAGE: Sculptor of the Harlem Renaissance

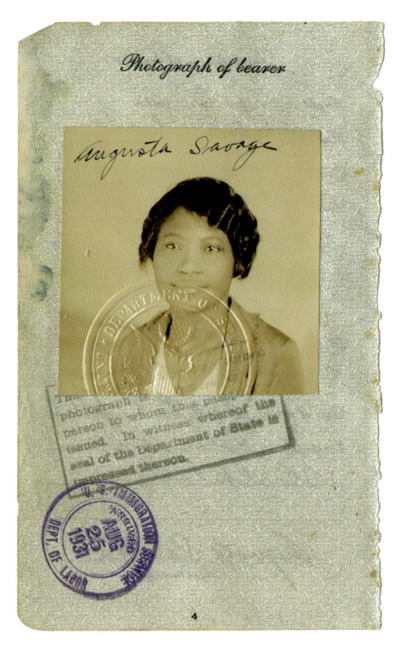

Though her time in Paris was relatively short, Savage absorbed the surrounding culture and used it for inspiration.

Making Friends in Paris

Paris was not spectacularly beautiful during the 1930s. The City on the Seine had, if anything, a rather drab look when compared to the romantic place we know today. But there was a strong community of African American expatriates; composed of about four hundred individuals, many of whom were interested in dance, song, and the visual arts, the African American community was lively and vibrant. Savage became firm friends with Countee Cullen, the brilliant poet who married the daughter of W. E. B. Du Bois.

Terpsichore (*Reclining Woman*), it seems reasonable to conclude that Savage was inspired by such dance performances.

Terpsichore's current location is unknown, but photographs from the early 1930s show that Savage sculpted a young woman in the nude, whose legs are crossed in such a manner as to hide her face as well as her private parts. At first this seems like modesty, but the viewer soon realizes this is an exaggerated dance pose. Better known is *La Citadelle—Freedom*, sculpted sometime in 1930.

In *La Citadelle—Freedom*, the figure is only 12 or 13 inches (30 to 33 cm) in height, but the exuberant, even extravagant, pose of the dancer draws our attention. Sculpted in bronze, *La Citadelle* shows a woman in the middle of a movement that suggests—though it does not confirm—ballet. Like many of Savage's figures, *La Citadelle* lacks color and therefore contrast. But the woman herself is compelling. One is tempted to read a message into the construction of the fluid lines of the figure, drawing the conclusion that Savage had indeed found freedom in Paris.

It was about this time—the height of Savage's overseas success—that a French periodical paid her special attention. The *African Dispatch* editors noted that Paris had many artists of color—musicians, dancers, singers, and painters—but that Augusta Savage was, quite possibly, the first African American sculptor to dwell in the City of Lights. Recounting Savage's long, and often tragic, personal history, the French periodical reproduced several of her works, notably *Gamin*.[2] The essay ended on an upbeat note: Savage seemed destined to show the Old World what African Americans could accomplish.

Praise for Savage's impressive work also traveled across the Atlantic. A Rosenwald Foundation official, George Robert Arthur, wrote directly to Savage: "I hope you will continue to work primarily with Negro models. I hope also that you will try to develop something original, born out of a deep spirituality which you, as a Negro woman, must feel in depicting modern Negro subjects. I even hope that you will not become too much imbued with European standards of technique, if they are going to kill the other something which in my opinion some Negro will eventually give to American art."[3] Arthur went on to write that African Americans were rapidly gaining in artistic expression and the only way to go "wrong" was to copy, or imitate, other people's standards of success. These were, quite likely, some of the most gratifying words Augusta Savage ever heard.

She thanked Arthur, writing that she was glad that they shared a singular opinion on the topic.

Savage's success in Paris raises one question: if she was doing so well in the City of Lights, why did she return to America? With the onset of the Great Depression in 1929, family ties and financial concerns conspired to pull Savage back to Manhattan. Her fellowship was renewed once, but when those funds were depleted, she simply had to return to the United States.

Chapter

8

Teacher and Mentor

Savage left for France in the very season—autumn of 1929—that the Great Depression began. A huge fall in stock market prices in October and November of 1929 led to prolonged economic weakness as well as the complete collapse of numerous businesses. Because she was in France for nearly two years, Savage was shielded from some of the Depression's worst effects, at least until she came home.

The Great Depression Hits Harlem

By 1932, Harlem had again become home to Augusta Savage. She might have been born and raised in Florida and never forgot her southern roots, but she had become a thoroughly urban and northern person. And with its influx of black artists, musicians, and writers, Harlem had embraced the person she was destined to become. But even while it remained rich in art, Harlem inevitably suffered from the effects of the Great Depression.

Harlem and its residents had long known hard times, so the first year of the Great Depression did not make visible changes to the neighborhood. But as the

Teacher and Mentor 65

Savage continued to sculpt in the 1930s, but she also expanded to mentoring local young artists in Harlem.

Depression continued, the economic circumstances of the neighborhood and its residents grew worse. Employment discrimination was always a matter of course for black men and women in the United States, but the extreme poverty that came with the Depression made the financial prospects of black Americans substantially worse. By the time Augusta Savage returned from Paris, Harlem was in a bad way.

The local press picked up on the disparity in circumstances between black citizens in Europe and in America. In response to a question by the *New York Amsterdam News*, Savage confirmed that the Depression was not nearly as bad in Paris as America.

> "It is no uncommon sight to see fifteen men employed at a job which could be handled competently by one man. This does not speak well for the efficiency of the French people, but it does go far to relieve suffering in that country."[1]

In response to another question, Savage replied:

> "Contrary to reports, there seems to be very little increase in race prejudice in Paris. Of course, the French hate the American whites, but there is little evidence that this hostility extends to the Negroes."[2]

While she could identify the struggles her fellow black Americans were suffering, money—either the making or conserving of it—had never been Savage's strong point. She had no remedy, either for her own situation or that of her people. She, therefore, turned her hand to the one thing she did know: the making of art.

The Renaissance and the Depression

While many black artists flowered during the period of the Harlem Renaissance, the Depression undoubtedly had a critical effect on the movement. As did nearly everyone in this time, the supporters and patrons of artists found themselves struggling to earn a living and passed that struggle along as they could not afford to buy artwork. There was no longer any such thing as "disposable" income. All money, whatever little was available, was directed at day-to-day survival. Some artists, like poet Langston Hughes, chose to leave as the early years of the 1930s forced the once vibrant city into a steep decline. The nearest thing to an official end of the Harlem Renaissance came with the Harlem Riot of 1935, a race riot seemingly sparked by a teenager's theft of a penknife but that reflected a deeper conflict caused by racial tension, the unemployment crisis, and a distrust of the police force.

An Open Studio

Savage still had her mother and several other relatives at her home. The Harlem apartment was jam-packed most of the time, but Savage also found the time and energy to bring in neighborhood youths. Nearly all of them were African American teenagers, and some of their lives echoed the streetwise look of *Gamin*, her sculpture from 1928. One such teenager was Norman Lewis.

68 **AUGUSTA SAVAGE:** *Sculptor of the Harlem Renaissance*

Landscape painter Norman Lewis found inspiration and creative courage in Augusta Savage's example.

Norman Lewis walked the streets of Harlem regularly, and one evening he saw a middle-aged black woman sculpting in her basement. He knocked on the door, asked what she was doing, and was soon recruited as her newest protégée. Raised in a middle-class home, Lewis was appalled by the grime and dust he encountered in that basement studio. In an oral history taped decades later, he recalled how he and Savage labored many hours to clean up the place.

Lewis later became a landscape painter, and he was sometimes asked whether Savage led him in that direction. No, Lewis replied, his artistic bent came from within. Rather, it was the inspiration of seeing an African American woman, one who clearly was accustomed to long hours and hard work, pursuing her own artistic dream—*that* was what gave him inspiration.[3]

There were plenty of other young teenagers in the neighborhood, and they crowded Savage's life. She never complained of this, however; and when she was interviewed by her brother-in-law, she had this to say: "I have created nothing really beautiful, really lasting, but if I can inspire one of these youngsters to develop the talent I know they possess, then my monument will be in their work."[4]

Adult Learners

Savage also aspired to reach adult learners, those who had never really given themselves a chance to succeed in the making of art. Perhaps the most well known of her adult students was Kenneth B. Clark. Years later, Clark, who eventually made his name as a researcher in child psychology, described his pivotal experience with Savage:

70 AUGUSTA SAVAGE: *Sculptor of the Harlem Renaissance*

> "I was [working on] this nude," Clark told Jervis Anderson, "and was having trouble with the breasts. Gwendolyn Knight [who developed into a fine artist] was sitting next to me, and I kept looking at her, to see whether I could make a breast that looked like a breast. Gwen knew what I was doing, but she would not help me. Augusta came along and said, 'Kenneth, you're having trouble with that breast.' I said, 'Yes, I am. And she simply opened her blouse and showed me her breast."[5]

It's clear that Savage possessed little ego about doing what was necessary to help her students expand their artistic capabilities. Perhaps it was because she believed in the quality of the artists she chose to mentor. As Romare Bearden and Harry Henderson, who studied her for many years, noted, "She attracted the gifted like the Pied Piper."[6] She likely didn't take that responsibility lightly.

A New Role

One of the most exciting and triumphant days of Savage's life came on December 20, 1937. On that date, the Harlem Community Art Center was formally opened. As director of this brand-new institution, Savage was the star of the show. But that day, she shared the stage with First Lady Eleanor Roosevelt and union leader Asa Philip Randolph.

The First Lady was already known as the best friend African Americans had within the Roosevelt administration. Mrs. Roosevelt gave a short but rousing speech, in which she hailed the new arts center as a "splendid enterprise,"[7] a huge step forward. Randolph, president of the Brotherhood of Sleeping Car Porters, gave a longer speech, enthusing

Teacher and Mentor 71

In addition to sculpture, Savage also occasionally dabbled in painting, but by the 1930s, she was setting aside her art to focus more on mentorship.

about art and what it meant for the African American community.

"The Negro people of Harlem look at art," Randolph declared. "They turn to culture. It is not the superficial striving for the unreal nor the un-purposeful effort for an exotic condition."[8] No, Randolph declared, art was the best medium for African Americans to show their special offerings to the world.

Savage was not interviewed that afternoon. But the chances are that this was one of the greatest, perhaps even sublime, moments of her entire life. Though she had experienced much hardship and adversity, she was the person most responsible for the rise of this new organization.

But whether Savage realized it or not, the formal organization of what she had previously been doing all on her own meant that dealing with federal bureaucracy was inevitable. It validated the importance of the work she had been doing with young men and women of Harlem, but it also signaled that she would no longer have complete control over the way she mentored would-be artists. For a stubborn soul like Savage, it would be her undoing.

Enemies in the Ranks

With her direct and occasionally abrasive style, Savage created almost as many enemies as admirers. She was no longer running her own private colony of artists over which she had sole control, and her lack of diplomacy soon tripped her up. In 1939, she was ousted from her position as director of the Harlem Community Artists Center.

Teacher and Mentor   73

Savage was so well known and so popular within her circle of artists, that it seemed almost impossible to push her out the door. But the federal board that oversaw the National Works Project found a pretext. When Savage accepted the prestigious commission to execute a piece of sculpture for the upcoming New York World's Fair, her foes declared that she was no longer a federal employee, that she had forfeited her position. Gwendolyn Bennett was appointed the new director. To say that Savage felt betrayed is an understatement. She had given her talent, time, and spirit to shaping these young men and women and was casually tossed aside for her troubles.

Chapter 9

The World's Fair

The New York World's Fair opened on April 30, 1939, the 150th anniversary of George Washington's inauguration as first president of the United States. A colossal statue of the first president greeted fair visitors, but the thousands of booths focused on the present and the promise of the future. The theme was "Building the World of Tomorrow."

Thirty-three states had their own pavilions, as did dozens of foreign nations. More than 1,200 acres (485 hectares) of land were used for the sprawling fair, which was expected to surpass all previous World's Fairs. While futuristic technologies, including early television sets and fancy automobiles, grabbed much attention, it has to be said that plenty of time and attention was devoted to the fine arts. Over 1,100 paintings were exhibited, as were more than 250 pieces of sculpture.

No one anticipated that Augusta Savage's sculpture would draw much attention. Her work competed with much larger and grander pieces of art. But there was something soulful and compelling about *The Harp*, which was placed directly outside the main entrance to the Building of Contemporary Arts.

Inspired by a Friend

Savage spent more than a year working on *The Harp*, also known as *Lift Every Voice and Sing*. She based this, her largest single piece of art, on a famous song written by a personal friend.

James Weldon Johnson grew up physically proximate to Augusta Savage, but their early lives could not have been more different. Unlike Savage who endured beatings from her father, Johnson grew up in a household that adored the arts. Born and raised in Jacksonville, Florida, less than a dozen miles from Green Cove Springs, Johnson and his younger brother, John Rosamond Johnson, were teachers in the local schools, and it is possible that this is when Johnson first met Augusta Savage.

Johnson described the conception of the song that became known as the Negro National Anthem: "A group of young men in Jacksonville, Florida, arranged to celebrate Lincoln's birthday in 1900. My brother, J. Rosamond Johnson and I decided to write a song to be sung at the exercises. I wrote the words and he wrote the music."[1] Both brothers soon moved from the Jacksonville area, and years passed, during which they seldom, if ever, thought about that song. "But the school children of Jacksonville kept singing it," Johnson wrote, "they went off to other schools and sang it; they became teachers and taught it to other children."[2] By 1939, "Lift Every Voice and Sing" was known throughout the United States.

To honor the Johnson brothers and to celebrate the importance of music to African Americans, Savage executed a 16-foot-high (5 meter) sculpture. The frame of the piece is the hand of God, which stretches forth to hold no fewer than twelve singers, who appear in ascending order, according to size. Every mouth is open, every face reflects purpose and joy, and the sculpture commemorates the happiness that can exist even in the presence of great pain.

Savage had experienced plenty of difficult press, but *The Harp* was a noteworthy exception. Not only did the piece receive substantial praise, the critics may even have overlooked certain flaws in the design, out of deference to its strikingly original conception. The real test lay with parents and children, however. How would they react?

Thousands, perhaps even tens of thousands, of families paused outside the Building of Contemporary Arts. Many photographed their children in front of *The Harp*. A majority of the families that passed through the fair's gates were white, and *The Harp* may have served as an introduction to the African American experience. To be sure, there was some sadness associated with the sculpture: Johnson, the man who did so

The World's Fair   77

Appearing at the 1939 World's Fair in New York, *The Harp* is Augusta Savage's most ambitious and well-known work.

James Weldon Johnson

One of the most prolific African American writers of his time, James Weldon Johnson thrived in Harlem, where he was the unofficial dean of the black intellectual scene. During his life, he held a number of professions; from songwriter to journalist to educator to diplomat, his talent truly ran the gamut. Johnson died in an automobile accident in Wiscasset, Maine, in 1938, one year before Augusta Savage's sculpture honored him, his brother, and the unofficial Negro National Anthem.

much to inspire its creation, died a year before the World's Fair opened.

The Second Run

The New York World's Fair opened to great fanfare in April 1939. Millions of people came to view the exhibits, but even with the ticket price set at 75 cents, not enough money was made to break even. Fair organizers made a second attempt in 1940. This time, fair admission was set at 50 cents.

The Harp was seen by hundreds of thousands of people in total. Savage received very good press for her work, but when the fair closed, in the autumn of 1940, she faced a painful decision: would she store *The Harp*, which was cast in plaster?

The World's Fair   79

Sadly, Augusta Savage didn't have the financial means to store *The Harp*, so it was destroyed in 1940, after the World's Fair closed.

Lacking sufficient funds for storage, Savage abandoned *The Harp*, which was bulldozed when the fair closed its doors. Savage had already experienced plenty of adversity in life, but this—the destruction of her largest piece of art—had to be heartbreaking. It was about this time, as well, that Savage learned she would not be able to return to her position as director of the Harlem Community Arts Center.

The Salon

In 1939, the same year *The Harp* was first shown, Savage opened a gallery in Harlem: the Salon of Contemporary Negro Art. Many people, black and white, may have thought of something similar, but no other person could have pulled it off. Given that this was the same season as the positive reception of *The Harp*, it seemed possible Savage had finally turned the corner—that she could bask in the light of her success.

But it was not to be. The Salon of Contemporary Negro Art was open only a few months. A lack of sales forced its closure, later in 1939. It seemed as if Savage was doomed to be ahead of her time. If only she were born a decade later, some—perhaps even many—of the things she dreamed of would have come to pass. But even in spite of these setbacks, she still was not done.

A Touring Exhibit

In the spring and early summer of 1940, Savage went to several Midwestern cities. Bringing as much art as she and her friends could carry, Savage held exhibits in Chicago and

Gary, Indiana. She gave deeply personal talks, detailing her struggles in the pursuit of fine art. Thousands of African American school-aged children came to her talks. The end results were, again, disappointing. Savage hoped to persuade African Americans to purchase more art, but the great majority simply lacked funds.

The American Negro Exposition opened in July 1940. Savage's work was under-represented, and a younger sculptor, Elizabeth Catlett, won first prize. As Romare Bearden and Harry Henderson expressed it, "Savage felt rejected by her own people."[3] One small light shined in the darkness. Savage did not live long enough to see it burst into flame.

Savage did not know, could not know, how many young people were inspired by her 1940 Midwest tour. Decades later it was revealed that she had kindled a flame in certain young people. Perhaps the most outstanding was Murcie Poplar Lavender. The eighth-grade student at Indiana's Roosevelt High School in Gary was permanently altered by listening to Savage speak. Inspired by Savage's talk and her work, Lavender became a visual artist, founding the Gary Art Institute in 1963.[4]

Chapter 10

An Unusual Retirement

Without an available journal or other written record, it is impossible for even the best journalist or historian to declare that Savage "quit" on her life and career. Savage had always been too proud to complain about her circumstances, and friends often declared she seemed the same as ever. But it came as a surprise, even a shock, when she moved to upstate New York.

Sometime in 1945, Savage moved to Saugerties, a village on the western side of the Hudson River. Though Saugerties is separated from Manhattan by only a ninety-minute drive, the two places could not be more different.

Dutch and Anglo Neighbors

No one knows why Savage chose Saugerties. The nineteenth-century town may have reminded her of Green Cove Springs, her Florida home. Though there were rather few black men and women in Saugerties, Savage fit in surprisingly well. She lived just outside of town, on a road that has since been named in her honor. Biographers make much of the fact that her house had neither plumbing nor running water, but these were not significant hardships for Savage. She had grown up in similar circumstances. At least she now was free of the big city and its distractions.

Savage worked for a mushroom grower, and she taught art to village schoolchildren on an informal basis. Her own art production slowed dramatically.

Neighbors frequently asked Savage why she left Harlem. Her first answer was always the same. The noise and bustle of the city interrupted her work, she said. But when people pressed and asked follow-up questions, Savage often gave a more detailed, and one suspects, a fuller answer. Communists had infiltrated many of the arts organizations, she said, and she did not wish to be affiliated with them. During the 1950s, this was a very satisfactory and "safe" answer in that Americans—whether urban or rural—tended to harbor a deep fear of communists. But Savage gave almost no one the third part of the formula. Virtually no one knew that relentless sexual harassment was another reason she fled the big city for the quiet countryside.

The Ugly Truth

After her husband and newborn daughter died in 1924, Savage continued to attend virtually all major gatherings of artists and writers in Harlem. At one of these—the precise date and place are unknown—she attracted the person who would become her number one predator. His name was Joe Gould, and he fell in love with her at first sight.

Joe Gould was considered a harmless eccentric, an insanely ambitious person who told anyone and everyone

Leaving New York City behind, Savage settled in the upstate New York town of Saugerties.

he was writing an oral history of twentieth-century life. There was some truth to the assertion—Gould did compile numerous manuscripts, always written in longhand. But if New York City life of the 1930s and 1940s was his literary obsession, then his physical appetite had long since settled on Augusta Savage.

An Unusual Retirement

An attractive and creative woman, Savage was someone who could lug plaster and stone if she wanted and who could also turn herself out in party clothing that admitted her to any social occasion. She had physical presence. Gould was immediately smitten with her.

Joe Gould, by contrast, was long, lanky, and incredibly awkward: he seemed to constantly be tying his shoes or straightening his clothes. One thing Gould possessed was a social pedigree. He hailed from an old New England family, and he attended Harvard University. Quite possibly, Gould thought this would be enough to win Augusta Savage. His error was eventually revealed, and her rejection infuriated him. His admiration and affection for Savage eventually twisted into a narrow, narcissistic form of hate. The exact nature of their relationship, and the extent of the harassment, is unknown. But it is completely certain that Joe Gould frequently made Augusta Savage's life miserable, driving her out of New York City.

Her Last Years

Savage nearly disappeared from the historical record. One of the few exceptions to the general rule was the occasional visit paid by her brother-in-law, Ted Poston. The youngest child of the Poston family of eight, Ted had long been Augusta's favorite, and in the 1950s, he dropped in to visit whenever possible. Poston and his wife noted that Savage did not seem changed—she was still the life of the party

Elusive Justice

With our twenty-first-century sensibilities, we naturally ask, why didn't Savage go to the police about Joe Gould's harassment? It's possible that she would have been reluctant to involve law enforcement because, culturally, her Deep South background frowned on being a tattletale. But the more substantial answer is that Savage likely mistrusted the police. Her reaction was natural and was shared by most other Harlemites. They believed the police would side with a white defendant, almost every time.

when she desired. But most of the time, she preferred to be left alone.

Savage was diagnosed with cancer in 1960. Her daughter, Irene Moore, persuaded her to move to Brooklyn, where she could take care of her. Savage died on March 26, 1962.

For many years she was practically forgotten.

The Legacy of Augusta Savage

The execution of *Gamin* was surely the high point of Savage's career. With that one piece of sculpture, she established a claim to long-term recognition. At the same time, it has to be admitted that many of her other works never quite fulfilled their promise—that something was missing. Critics have long leveled a charge at Savage, that

An Unusual Retirement

Though she disappeared from the historical record for a time, Augusta Savage left a powerful legacy as a black artist.

AUGUSTA SAVAGE: Sculptor of the Harlem Renaissance

her work was spotty and uneven. There was the occasional triumph, such as *Gamin*, they declared, but Savage could have accomplished much more.

A second group of critics have long maintained that Savage would have done better to listen to older and wiser artists. She gave too much time and attention to the young, they declared, and thereby missed her own opportunities.

Both groups of critics are correct in the particulars and mistaken in the long-range view. Yes, Savage's work was extremely uneven. She attempted all sorts of sculptures— as well as poetry and even the writing of detective stories (none of them published)—and as a result she never gained a hard-core constituency, a group that would stick with her through thick and thin. And it is true that Savage gave too much to the younger generation through her mentorship instead of focusing on her own art. She herself agreed with that point; in an interview conducted by her brother-in-law Ted Poston, she claimed that she had not created anything really special in her own art. Her true legacy, she declared, was the work that would be produced by her students.

After all the disclaimers, one still faces the central question: did Savage do all she could, with the talent she possessed?

The answer is a resounding yes. Possessing but a smidgeon of formal training, Savage became *the* female African American sculptor of her time. The unevenness— one might say messiness—of her career reflects her brilliance. Her talent was too large to put in one place. She struggled with her art and the dilemmas posed by racism, sexism, even ageism, throughout her life—and she triumphed.

Chronology

1892

Augusta Fells is born in Green Cove Springs, Florida.

c. 1898

She begins to make clay pottery.

1907

She marries John Moore.

1908

Her daughter, Irene Moore, is born.

1908

John Moore dies.

1915

The Fells family moves south to West Palm Beach, Florida.

1919

Savage exhibits at the Palm Beach Fair.

1920

She lives in Jacksonville, Florida.

1921

Savage moves to New York City.

1922

She executes a bust of W. E. B. Du Bois.

1923

Savage begins a bust of Marcus Garvey; she exposes the racism of the Fontainebleau art committee; she marries Robert Poston.

1924

Poston dies on his way home from Africa; Savage brings his body to Hopkinsville, Kentucky; she gives birth to a girl, Roberta Poston, who dies days later.

1928

Savage's parents come north to live with her; she executes *Gamin*, her most fully realized work.

1929

Her father dies in a house fire; she wins a Rosenwald fellowship and departs for France; the Great Depression begins.

1930

Savage lives in Paris, studying briefly with a French master sculptor before going out on her own; her Rosenwald fellowship is renewed.

1931

Savage wins attention from the French press; she sculpts several figures based on stories about the Amazons.

1932

Savage returns to Harlem.

1933

Franklin Roosevelt's administration establishes the WPA, the Works Progress Administration.

1935

A major race riot explodes in Harlem, effectively ending the Harlem Renaissance.

1936

Franklin Roosevelt wins reelection by a landslide.

1937

Savage becomes head of the new Harlem Community Arts Center.

1939

The Harp is a major hit at the New York World's Fair.

1940

The Harp is demolished at the end of the second World's Fair season; Savage travels to Chicago and the Midwest.

1945

Savage leaves Harlem for Saugerties, NY, 100 miles (160 km) north along the Hudson River.

1960

Savage contracts cancer; someone steals her bust of W. E. B. Du Bois from the New York Public Library.

1962

Augusta Savage dies in New York City.

Chapter Notes

Chapter 1
Soft Florida Clay

1. Augusta Savage, "An Autobiography," *The Crisis* (August 1929), p. 269.
2. Ibid.
3. Ibid.
4. Kevin S. Hooper, *Green Cove Springs* (Charleston, SC: Arcadia Publishing, 2010).

Chapter 2
A Path Leading North

1. George Graham Currie, *Songs of Florida and Other Verse* (New York, NY: James T. White, 1922), p. 114.
2. Currie, p. 111.
3. Augusta Savage, "An Autobiography," *The Crisis* (August 1929), p. 269
4. Tony Martin, *African Fundamentalism: A Literary and Cultural Anthology of Garvey's Renaissance* (Dover, MA: Majority Press, 1984), p. 190.
5. Ibid.

Chapter 3
Schooling and Sculpting in New York City

1. Romare Bearden and Harry Henderson, *A History of African-American Artists from 1792 to the Present* (New York, NY: Pantheon Books, 1993).
2. Tony Martin, *African Fundamentalism: A Literary and Cultural Anthology of Garvey's Renaissance* (Dover, MA: Majority Press, 1984), p. 303.
3. Martin, p. 305.

AUGUSTA SAVAGE: Sculptor of the Harlem Renaissance

Chapter 4
A Rising Star

1. Romare Bearden and Harry Henderson, *A History of African-American Artists from 1792 to the Present* (New York, NY: Pantheon Books, 1993).
2. "Miss Savage Tells Story at Lyceum," *New York Amsterdam News* (May 16, 1923), p. 7.

Chapter 5
Heartbreak from Overseas

1. Kathleen A. Hauke, *Ted Poston: Pioneer American Journalist* (Athens, GA: University of Georgia Press, 1998).
2. Ibid.

Chapter 6
Harlem's Renaissance

1. W. E. B. Du Bois, "Criteria of Negro Art," *The Crisis* (October 1926), p. 294.
2. Ibid.

Chapter 7
An American in Paris

1. Theresa Leininger-Miller, *New Negro Artists in Paris: African American Painters and Sculptors in the City of Light, 1922–1934* (New Brunswick, NJ: Rutgers University Press, 2001).
2. Ibid.
3. Amy Helene Kirschke, *Women Artists of the Harlem Renaissance* (Jackson, MS: University Press of Mississippi, 2014).

Chapter 8
Teacher and Mentor

1. "Miss Augusta Savage Finds No Bread Line in Gay Paris," *New York Amsterdam News* (September 2, 1931), p. 3.
2. Ibid.

Chapter Notes   95

3. Oral Interview of Norman Lewis, conducted on July 14, 1968, found online at Archives of American art, www.aaa.si.edu/collections/interviews/oral-history.
4. T. R. Poston, "Augusta Savage," *Metropolitan Magazine* (January 1935).
5. Romare Bearden and Harry Henderson, *A History of African-American Artists from 1792 to the Present* (New York, NY: Pantheon Books, 1993), p. 179.
6. Ibid.
7. "Harlem's Art Center," *Art Digest* (January 1, 1938), p. 15.
8. Ibid.

Chapter 9

The World's Fair

1. James Weldon Johnson, *Writings* (New York, NY: Library of America, 2004).
2. Ibid.
3. Romare Bearden and Harry Henderson, *A History of African-American Artists from 1792 to the Present* (New York, NY: Pantheon Books, 1993), 179.
4. Anthony Kadarrell Thigpen, "The Gift Never Stops: Retired Art Teacher Helps Children Develop Their Talents," *Post-Tribune* (Gary, IN; September 26, 2003).

Glossary

Back to Africa A social movement originated by black leader Marcus Garvey, advocating for black American men and women to resettle in Africa.

black nationalism Belief system that promotes a separatist black nation and identity with the goal of escaping white supremacy.

City of Lights A nickname for Paris because of the many bridges and boulevards that are lit by over twenty thousand lamps.

disparity An inequality or difference between two things.

expatriate Someone who leaves their homeland to settle in a different country.

fundamentalist A person who takes an extremely strict view of a particular subject, usually religion.

grant Funding given to someone to allow him or her to begin or continue a project.

Great Depression An era between 1929 and 1939 marked by a nationwide economic crisis.

orator A speaker, particularly one who is gifted.

patrician Of or relating to a wealthy, well-connected family.

protégée Someone who studies with and learns from a mentor.

sojourn A temporary trip.

Ten Percent Concept promoted by W. E. B. Du Bois that exceptional black men and women (one in ten) would uplift the entire race.

urchin A child living in poverty.

Further Reading

BOOKS

Bearden, Romare, and Harry Henderson. *A History of African-American Artists from 1792 to the Present.* New York, NY: Pantheon Books, 1993.

Hayes, Jefreen, et al. *Augusta Savage: Renaissance Woman.* London, UK: Giles, 2018.

Hirschke, Amy Helene, ed. *Women Artists of the Harlem Renaissance.* Jackson, MS: University Press of Mississippi, 2014.

Schroeder, Alan, and JaeMe Bereal. *In Her Hands: The Story of Sculptor Augusta Savage.* New York, NY: Lee and Low Books, 2009.

WEBSITES

Augusta Savage–Smithsonian American Art Museum
https://americanart.si.edu/artist/augusta-savage-4269
A brief biography of Augusta Savage.

Meet Augusta Savage, the Most Important African-American Sculptor
https://vimeo.com/209768542
Video footage of Augusta Savage at work.

The Most Important Black Woman Sculptor of the 20th Century Deserves More Recognition
https://timeline.com/the-most-important-black-woman-sculptor-of-the-20th-century-deserves-more-recognition-af0ed7084bb1
An opinion piece on Savage's significance as a black female artist.

Index

A

Académie de la Grande Chaumière, 56
African Americans in the early twentieth century, 6, 9, 11, 16, 18, 21, 24, 27, 36–38, 41, 43, 45–46, 51, 55, 59, 61, 66
Arthur, George Robert, 62–63

B

Back to Africa movement, 34, 38, 41, 43
Bearden, Romare, 70, 81
Benneteau-Desgrois, Félix, 56–57
Borglum, Solon, 27

C

Clark, Kenneth B., 69–70
Cooper Union, 27–28
Crisis, The, 9, 24
Cullen, Countee, 61
Currie, George Graham, 15–17, 18, 27

D

Du Bois, W. E. B., 24, 32, 34, 45–48, 53, 61
	Savage's bust of, 28–30, 31, 45

views on art, 46–48, 51
Duncan, Isadora, 59

F

Fells, Edward (father), 8, 11, 12, 13, 20, 49, 75
Florida Normal Teachers College, 18
Fontainebleau School of Fine Arts, 36–38
fundamentalism, 8, 11

G

Gamin, 49–53, 62, 67, 86, 88
Garvey, Marcus, 32, 34, 36, 38, 39, 41, 43, 45
	Savage's bust of, 31, 32, 45
Gould, Joe, 83–85, 86
Great Depression, 63, 64–66, 67
Great Migration, 9, 19
Green Cove Springs, Florida, 6–8, 11–12, 13, 19, 75, 82

H

Harlem, New York, 21, 27, 32, 34, 36, 37, 39, 43, 53, 64–66, 67–73, 78, 83, 86
	Renaissance, 45, 67
Harlem Community Art Center, 70–73, 80

101

Harp, The, 74, 75–80
Henderson, Harry, 70, 81
Hughes, Langston, 53, 67

J

Jacksonville, Florida, 18, 19, 75
Johnson, James Weldon, 75, 76–78
Johnson, John Rosamond, 75

L

La Citadelle—Freedom, 61–62
Lavender, Murcie Poplar, 81
Lewis, Norman, 67–69
"Lift Every Voice and Sing," 75
Lincoln, Abraham, 53, 75

M

Moore, Irene (daughter), 11, 16, 17, 86
Moore, John (first husband), 11–12, 17

N

National Association for the Advancement of Colored People (NAACP), 46

P

Palm Beach County Fair, 13–14, 15–16
Paris, France, 24, 54, 55–63, 66
Poston, Roberta Savage (daughter), 44, 83
Poston, Robert L. (third husband), 36, 37, 38, 39
death of, 41–43, 44, 83
Poston, Ted, 43, 49, 69, 85, 88
propagandists and art, 48, 51
Prophet, Nancy Elizabeth, 55, 59
purists and art, 48, 51

R

Randolph, Asa Philip, 70–72
Reynolds, Kate L., 27, 28
Roosevelt, Eleanor, 70
Rosenwald, Julius, 53
Rosenwald Foundation and grant, 53, 54, 55, 56, 59, 62
Royal Academy of Fine Arts, 48

S

Salon of Contemporary Negro Art, 80
Saugerties, New York, 49, 82–83

Savage, Augusta
adult students of, 69–70
becomes a sculptor, 13,
16–20
childhood, 6–9, 11, 20
children of, 11, 16, 17, 39,
44, 45, 83, 86
at Cooper Union, 27–28
death of, 86
as director of Harlem
Community Art Center,
70–73, 80
early interest in sculpting,
8, 12, 20
Fontainebleau affair, 36–38
legacy, 86–88
marriages, 11–12, 13, 36,
38, 39, 41–44, 45
move to Saugerties, 82–83
in New York City, 9, 19,
21–31, 32, 36, 37, 39, 43,
45–49, 53, 63, 64, 67–73,
74–80, 83
opens salon, 80
in Paris, 24, 53–54, 55–63
poems, 16, 20
recognition and fame,
28–31, 32, 37–38, 39, 45,
46–54, 56–57, 61–63,
69, 70, 72–73, 74, 76, 78,
80–81, 86–88
touring exhibition, 80–81

World's Fair and, 73,
74–80
as youth mentor, 67–69, 88
Savage, James (second
husband), 13

T

Tanner, Henry O., 55
Terpsichore (Reclining Woman), 61

U

Universal Negro Improvement
League, 42, 43

W

Walrond, Eric, 30–31
West Palm Beach, Florida,
11–12, 13
World's Fair, 73, 74–80

Charlotte
Etinde-Crompton

Samuel
Willard Crompton

About the Authors

Charlotte Etinde-Crompton was born and raised in Zaire and came to Massachusetts at the age of twenty. Her artistic sensibility stems from her early exposure to the many talented artists of her family and tribe, which included master wood-carvers. Her interest in African American art has been an abiding passion since her arrival in the United States.

Samuel Willard Crompton is a tenth-generation New Englander who now lives in metropolitan Atlanta. For twenty-eight years, he was a professor of history at Holyoke Community College. His early interest in the arts came from his wood-carver father and his oil-painter mother. Crompton is the author and editor of many books, including a number of nonfiction young adult titles with Enslow Publishing. This is his first collaboration with his wife.